MAR 1 2

GUIDE
DOG
HEROES

Linda
Bozzo

Bailey Books
an imprint of
Enslow Publishers, Inc.
40 Industrial Road
Box 398
Berkeley Heights, NJ 07922
USA
http://www.enslow.com

This book is dedicated to Israel (Izzy) Bravo and his guide dog, Panzy.
May their love and devotion be an inspiration to others.

Founded in 1877, the American Humane Association is the only national organization dedicated to protecting both children and animals. Through a network of child and animal protection agencies and individuals, American Humane develops policies, legislation, curricula, and training programs—and takes action—to protect children and animals from abuse, neglect, and exploitation. To learn how you can support American Humane's vision of a nation where no child or animal will ever be a victim of abuse or neglect, visit www.americanhumane.org, phone (303) 792-9900, or write to the American Humane Association at 63 Inverness Drive East, Englewood, Colorado, 80112-5117.

AMERICAN HUMANE

Protecting Children & Animals Since 1877

Bailey Books, an imprint of Enslow Publishers, Inc.

Copyright © 2011 by Enslow Publishers, Inc.

Library of Congress Cataloging-in-Publication Data

Bozzo, Linda.

    Guide dog heroes / Linda Bozzo.

        p. cm. — (Amazing working dogs with American humane)

    Includes bibliographical references and index.

    Summary: "The text opens with a true story of a guide dog, and then it explains the history of guide dogs and the training methods used to transform an ordinary dog into a canine hero"—Provided by publisher.

    ISBN 978-0-7660-3198-2

    1. Guide dogs—Juvenile literature. I. Title.

    HV1780.B69 2011

    362.4'183—dc22   2009033877

Printed in China

052010 Leo Paper Group, Heshan City, Guangdong, China.

10 9 8 7 6 5 4 3 2 1

To Our Readers: We have done our best to make sure all Internet Addresses in this book were active and appropriate when we went to press. However, the author and the publisher have no control over and assume no liability for the material available on those Internet sites or on other Web sites they may link to. Any comments or suggestions can be sent by e-mail to comments@enslow.com or to the address on the back cover.

Every effort has been made to locate all copyright holders of material used in this book. If any errors or omissions have occurred, corrections will be made in future editions of this book.

Illustration Credits: Associated Press, pp. 40, 42; Linda Bozzo, pp. 20, 24; Courtesy of Israel Bravo, pp. 6, 8, 10; Nicole diMella/Enslow Publishers, Inc., pp. 1, 26, 29, 31, 41; Courtesy of Michael Hingson, p. 44; © Peter Hvizdak/The Image Works, p. 37; © iStockphoto.com/Katherine Moffitt, p. 18 (bottom); © iStockphoto.com/Petr Koudelka, p. 19; © Journal Courier/Steve Warmowski/The Image Works, p. 34; © 2009 Jupiterimages Corporation, p. 18 (top); © Tony Savino/The Image Works, p. 36; Shutterstock, p. 4; © Syracuse Newspapers/S Cannerelli/The Image Works, p. 23; Courtesy of The Seeing Eye, pp. 12, 15, 16; Jonathan Wiggs/Boston Globe/Landov, p. 38.

Cover Illustration: Courtesy of The Seeing Eye.

Contents

Thank You

Enslow Publishers, Inc. would like to thank The Seeing Eye in Morristown, New Jersey, for advising us on this manuscript. A special thank you for taking the time to meet with us and allowing us to photograph at The Seeing Eye.

The author would also like to thank Teresa Davenport at The Seeing Eye for all of her help with this project. The author would also like to thank her friend Noelle, who was training a dog for The Seeing Eye, for sharing her experiences with her dog, Leslie.

Panzy
A True Story

Like many students, Israel Bravo attended college after high school. It was not surprising that Izzy, as his friends call him, found college to be a challenge. There was a new schedule, new friends, and a school that he was not familiar with. But Izzy had one more challenge. He was blind. Blind since birth, Izzy had always been comfortable using a cane to get around. But at college, Izzy was beginning to feel that the cane was not enough.

Izzy and his guide dog Panzy

The college Izzy was attending did not have Braille signs outside the classroom doors. Braille is a series of raised dots that serves as a written alphabet for the blind. He often had to ask other students to help him find his classrooms. The small room he lived in with other students made it hard for him to get around. His roommates moved things around a lot. "Even with my cane I was always bumping into things," he said.

After several months at college, Izzy was still having a hard time with his new surroundings. Back in high school, Izzy participated in a program that helped blind students prepare for college. This program allowed him to actually try using a guide dog. He had always heard and read about guide dogs. At the time, Izzy thought it would be too hard to take care of a dog. "Having a guide dog is a huge responsibility," Izzy remembered thinking. But after the difficulties he was experiencing, he decided he needed more help. He hoped a guide dog would be the answer to his problem. So Izzy decided to train with a guide dog during his winter break from school.

Since he was young Izzy felt he needed a dog that would be okay with his busy life. He needed a dog

Panzy helps Izzy cross the street.

that would be compatible with his personality. Izzy was partnered with a female black Labrador retriever named Panzy. Panzy turned out to be the perfect match. After spending a month training with his guide dog, Izzy returned to school. It was difficult at first. It took some time for Panzy to understand he was her new handler. Once he started taking care of Panzy they began to bond. Izzy really liked knowing Panzy was there watching him all the time.

"I used to have to ask people where everything was," Izzy explained. "After just a few days, Panzy became familiar with my routine." Izzy could start walking in the direction of the cafeteria or the library, then Panzy would guide him the rest of the way. Izzy no longer had to worry if he was going to the wrong classroom or where the library was. "I could direct her toward the library and she would guide me there." During class, Panzy would lie between Izzy's legs under his desk and rest.

Panzy also made traveling easier for Izzy. He used to hate riding the subway, train, and bus. "Panzy changed all that. She made it easy to get around." Panzy learned which train they needed to take to get back to school. She even knew which stop they needed to get off at. Izzy no longer had to depend

Izzy is very thankful to have Panzy in his life.

on his parents for rides. Panzy gave Izzy freedom he had never known before. "Because of Panzy, I was able to get a job for the first time." Izzy was even able to travel on airplanes with Panzy.

Today Panzy goes everywhere with Izzy. She even goes with him and his friends to baseball and basketball games. She travels on airplanes with him too. "With a guide dog, you never feel like you are alone." Having a guide dog helps make Izzy feel sure of himself. "Panzy makes it all easier. Having a guide dog is life changing. It is just really amazing."

Chapter 1

The History of Guide Dogs

ogs have helped guide people who are blind or visually impaired for many years. Guide dogs help people who cannot see by guiding them safely from place to place. This allows blind people to live a more independent life.

No one knows exactly when dogs began guiding people. It is known that the Germans trained German shepherd dogs to guide soldiers that were blinded in World War I. In the 1920s, Dorothy Harrison Eustis,

Dorothy Harrison Eustis with a German shepherd in Switzerland.

an American woman living in Switzerland, was a German shepherd breeder and trainer of working dogs. Ms. Eustis learned of several schools in Germany that were training dogs to guide soldiers and others who were blind. She visited one school in Potsdam, Germany, that inspired her to write a magazine article describing what she saw. Her article titled "The Seeing Eye" appeared in the magazine the *Saturday Evening Post* on November 5, 1927. Ms. Eustis spoke about the idea of a blind person being led across a busy street. Ms. Eustis wrote: "The future for all blind men can be the same, however blinded. No longer dependent on a member of the family, a friend or a paid attendant, the blind can once more take up their normal lives as nearly as possible where they left them off."

Many people read Ms. Eustis's article. She received lots of letters, including one from a young blind man living in Tennessee named Morris Frank. Mr. Frank longed to regain some of the independence he had lost since being blinded several years earlier. In his letter, he asked Ms. Eustis if she could teach him how to use a guide dog. Mr. Frank wrote: "Train me and I will bring back my dog and show people here how a blind man can be absolutely on his own."

Touched by the blind man's letter, Ms. Eustis agreed to help him. She spent time training several dogs, including a female German shepherd named Kiss. In 1928, when the dogs were ready, she invited Mr. Frank to Switzerland. It was there that Mr. Frank learned how to use Kiss, whom he soon renamed Buddy. They practiced walking busy streets, shops, and even stairways. Finally Mr. Frank was able to go places he could not go before by himself. After finishing their six-week training in Switzerland, Mr. Frank and Buddy returned to the United States. The guide dog and his blind master traveled the country together. As promised, Mr. Frank showed others how Buddy could help guide him. He spread the word about how dogs could make a difference in the lives of people who are blind.

In Nashville, Tennessee, on January 29, 1929, Ms. Eustis along with Mr. Frank founded The Seeing Eye, a guide dog school. A few years later, The Seeing Eye moved to Morristown, New Jersey.

In February 1930, Helen Keller, a blind and deaf woman, visited The Seeing Eye. In a letter following her visit, Ms. Keller wrote: "Only since the World War have dogs been accorded their rightful place in service and friendship. The door of opportunity

In 1927, Dorothy Eustis wrote an article that was published in the *Saturday Evening Post*.

This is Morris Frank and his guide dog Buddy.

was opened to them when Germany began to educate them as guides for blinded soldiers."

Over the years, guide dog schools have opened all over the world. About ten thousand people in the United States and Canada use guide dogs. The skills these dogs learn enable the blind community to be successful in whatever they set out to do. These highly trained animals are heroes that help change the lives of the people they guide.

Chapter 2

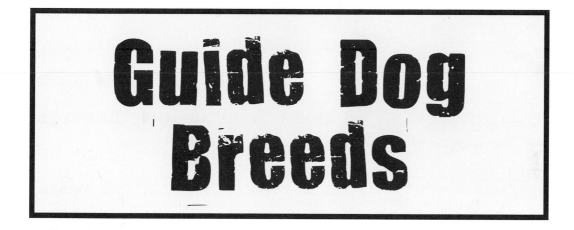

Guide Dog Breeds

Guide dogs guide their blind partners through places like busy streets and malls. They lead them up and down curbs and around obstacles. Guide dogs guide their blind partners safely through their lives daily. This is an important job. Therefore, the breed of dog is important.

Guide dogs must be smart and eager to work. They should be friendly and alert. That is why German shepherds, Labrador retrievers, golden retrievers, and

German shepherd (top) and Labrador retriever (bottom).

mixes of the breeds are popular choices. These breeds have also proven that they are easy to train and willing to work.

Size is important for guide dogs. A guide dog must be large enough to keep up with her partner when walking. Yet she needs to be small enough to fit easily under a table at a restaurant or under a seat on a bus. That is why these medium-sized breeds make good guide dogs. Strength is also important. These breeds are gentle but tend to be strong enough to pull their partners away from danger if they have to. Male and female dogs make equally excellent guide dogs.

When matching a guide dog with a blind person, the dog's personality traits are more important than the dog's breed or where the dog comes from. Guide dogs and their partners work together as a team. It is best that the dog suits her partner's personality and her physical needs.

Golden retriever

Puppy raisers are very important.

Chapter 3

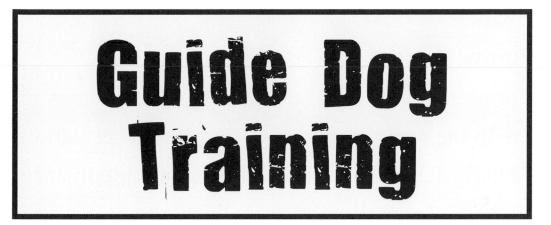

Guide Dog Training

Like other working dogs, guide dogs need to be properly trained. Although there are many different guide dog schools, most train their dogs in similar ways.

Most guide dog schools prefer to breed their own dogs. This means that the puppies are born at the school. When the puppies are around two months old, they leave the school to live with volunteer foster families. These families, also known as puppy raisers, provide loving homes while they teach and care for the puppies until they are around twelve months old or so.

Puppy Raisers

During the first year of the puppy's life, he learns to live in the world around him. He learns to be part of a family. Puppies need lots of love and attention to grow into happy, healthy guide dogs.

Puppy raisers and their puppies attend classes together. The puppies learn simple obedience commands like sitting, lying down, and staying in place when told. Through obedience lessons good manners are taught. Good manners include no jumping or barking, biting, sniffing, or even begging.

During training, it is sometimes necessary to repeat a task until the dog gets it right. Lots of praise, playtime, and petting are successful rewards.

It is the puppy raiser's job to show the puppy the world in which he will someday work. This means taking the puppy for car rides and trips to places like the mall. Puppies need to get used to being around noises and people. This is called socialization. "I take my puppy, Leslie, to the library for socialization,"

Dogs that are training to be guide dogs, must get used to different places. This girl brings the dog to school.

Noelle, who is a puppy raiser, explains. "She loves to be pet by the children while I read to them."

The puppy raiser will take the puppy on outings in order to get him used to walking on a leash. Puppies should also get used to walking on different surfaces, like the slippery floor of a store.

The puppy raiser is also responsible for raising a strong, healthy dog. This means brushing and grooming the dog's coat to keep it clean and shiny. She will need to make sure the dog has clean water to drink and is fed only at scheduled

Dogs that may make good guide dogs live with a special puppy raiser. The puppy raiser will take the puppy on outings to get him used to people and noise.

times. Noelle admits that this can be difficult with three other dogs in her house. "Leslie must be fed separately from the other dogs. It is important that she is fed at the same time every day." Puppies should be taken for walks and given plenty of exercise. Visits to the veterinarian and vaccinations are important to raising a healthy puppy.

The puppy will stay with the foster family until he or she is around fourteen to eighteen months old. "Being a puppy raiser takes lots of time and is very hard work," Noelle admits. "But it is worth it to help a blind person."

Formal Training

From the foster family's home, the dog returns to the school for formal training with an instructor.

The instructor's job is to prepare the dogs for their work as guide dogs.

They start with basic skills and move to more advanced ones.

During this time, the dog also begins to wear a harness. A guide dog's harness is a set of leather straps with a U-shaped handle and a leash that the blind

Formal training means that the dog works with a guide dog trainer. The trainer trains the dog to get used to busy streets.

person holds to connect her to the dog. While in harness, the dog learns commands like right, left, and forward. This teaches the dog to walk in different directions.

Other skills the dogs are taught include how to lead their instructor safely around an obstacle or object that is in the way. The dogs are taught to stop for obstacles overhead as well, like tree branches. They learn to stop for curbs, stairs, and other changes in their path. Guide dogs cannot understand signs or traffic lights, but they can see cars coming. They learn not to obey a handler's command if they see danger, such as a speeding car. During skill training, dogs are taught to avoid distractions like cats or squirrels. They need to give their full attention to their partner's needs.

Formal training usually starts in a quiet setting. By the end of training, dogs are taken to busy streets and sidewalks. Instructors get the dogs used to riding public transportation, like city buses, subways, and trains. They are taught to ride quietly, lying down under a seat when possible.

Rewards of praise are used to train a happy working dog. Harder tasks may require that the instructor make corrections. The instructor may need to repeat the task over and over until the dog gets it right.

Formal training usually lasts around four months. If the instructor thinks the dog is ready, the dog is tested. Once the dog passes testing, he or she will be matched with a person who is blind or visually impaired. What a reward!

Partner Training

A person who chooses to use a guide dog for mobility must first be matched with their new partner. When matching a person with a dog, the trainer must think

Once the dog is ready, he is paired with his partner. The dog and partner work with the trainer.

about both of their personalities. The trainer will consider their sizes, the pace at which they both walk, and their personalities.

During this time, the dog and her partner begin to learn to trust each other and work together as a team. Partner training takes around one month.

They learn to travel safely together down crowded sidewalks and across busy streets. A guide dog handler must know the direction to travel in order to get to where he wants to go. The handler is taught to direct the dog using voice commands the dog has already learned. Using the handle of the harness, a blind person learns to follow the way his dog moves around obstacles. This can be difficult at first. Over time, the handler learns to trust the guidance of his dog. They practice in different surroundings, like beaches, city streets, and shopping centers. They will learn to ride escalators and elevators together.

The trainer works with the dog and his partner in shopping malls, in stores, and many other places.

During partner training, they will ride buses, taxis, and even the subway. The handler will also learn to stop or slow down when his dog stops or slows down.

It is important that the handler learns how to care for his dog. After all, they will be partners for many years.

When partner training is completed, the guide dog and his or her blind partner graduate from training school. The guide dog is ready to do her job, leading her partner everywhere they go.

Not every dog is successful as a guide dog. "If I feel the dog just needs more time, I will take him back for extra training," one instructor explains. But if a dog does not qualify for guide work, that is okay. Many dogs work doing search and rescue or pet therapy. Some even go on to work as service dogs. The dog may be adopted by his puppy raiser or another loving family.

Some reasons why dogs may leave a program:

- Nervousness
- Distractibility
- Fear
- Unhappiness with work
- Medical reasons

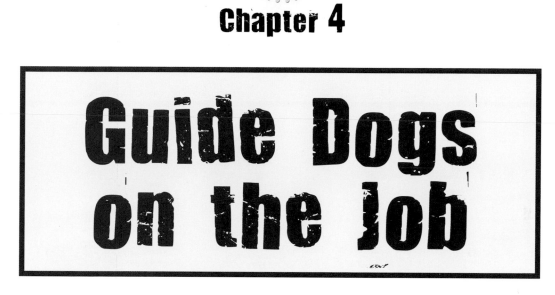

Chapter 4

Guide Dogs on the Job

After returning home, the guide dog and his blind partner will travel everywhere together. Their bond becomes stronger. They blend their skills to work together. Over time, they adjust to each other. Soon it will be hard for them to imagine life without each other.

When you see a working guide dog, it is important to speak to the handler and not the dog. Speaking to or petting the dog will keep him from doing his job.

This could put the dog and the handler in danger. It is always best to ask the handler's permission before petting or speaking to the guide dog.

Guide dogs go everywhere with their partners—even grocery stores!

It is the handler's job to direct the dog where he or she wants to go. The handler will use commands like "forward," "right," "left," and others.

A guide dog is often seen working with his or her partner on busy streets. When the team comes to a corner, the dog will stop. The handler must listen for the sounds of traffic or any other sounds that say it is not safe to cross. When the handler feels it is safe, then he or she will give the dog the command to move forward. If it is not safe to move forward, it is the dog's job to not

This college student uses her guide dog around campus.

obey the command. This is called "intelligent disobedience."

It is the guide dog's job to lead his partner around obstacles so she does not get hurt. When a dog comes to an obstacle, he will stop. This tells his blind partner that there is an obstacle, like a tree or a bush.

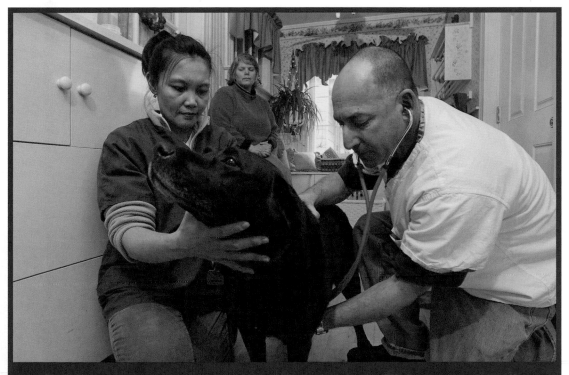

Guide dogs need to go to the vet, too. This vet actually goes to the person's house to give the dog a check-up.

The handler's job is to care for her dog. She must exercise, feed, and groom her dog. The handler must take her dog to the veterinarian when needed.

Guide dogs go wherever their partner goes. They must be comfortable on subways!

A guide dog even works at night. The dog will sleep in his partner's bedroom. If the blind person needs to get up, the dog must be there, ready to work.

When the harness is off, guide dogs love to play just like any pet. Whether at work or play, a blind person finds it hard to remember her life without her guide dog. The dog and handler have become a team that will work and play together for many years to come.

Chapter 5

When Guide Dogs Retire

s with other working dogs, there comes a time when a guide dog retires, or no longer works. Most guide dogs work for around eight years, but every dog is different. Some dogs may work for ten years or more.

It is often hard to retire a guide dog, but what is best for the dog comes first. Retired guide dogs may be kept by their partners as pets. For some dogs this may be a challenge. A dog can become jealous or

Guide dogs lead a hard, but productive life.

even feel sad if her partner brings a new guide dog into the home.

A retired guide dog can also be adopted, sometimes by her partner's family or a friend. Often, a retired dog is returned to her puppy raiser family, the home in which she was raised. Much care is taken to make sure that a dog retires to a loving home. The end of her working life is really a new beginning.

When a dog is ready, she retires from being a guide dog. A loving family can adopt retired guide dogs.

Guide dogs
are heroes!

Chapter 6

Guide Dogs Are Heroes

On September 11, 2001, Michael Hingson was in his office on the seventy-eighth floor of Tower One in the World Trade Center. When an airplane hijacked by terrorists hit the tower just fifteen floors above his office, Hingson realized something was terribly wrong. He heard a loud noise; he felt the building moving. He smelled smoke in the air. What Hingson was not able to do was see. Hingson is blind. He would need the help of his guide dog,

Michael Hingson used his guide dog to help him down the stairs.

Roselle, to escape the building safely. Hingson directed Roselle to an emergency exit. The dog then guided Hingson down the crowded stairwell. They worked as a team to make it outside alive. With the help of his guide dog, Michael Hingson was able to escape the building safely.

Guide dogs, like Roselle, are heroes that can save lives. These loving animals help give people who are blind opportunities they might never have had. These heroes are often seen guiding their partners at work or school. They enjoy visits to stores, restaurants, and many other places. These heroes guide their partners in their everyday travels, keeping them away from danger.

With guide dogs at their sides, blind men and woman are given new lives filled with freedom.

Glossary

Braille—Raised dots that represent writing for the blind.

breed—A certain type of dog; to raise certain types of dogs.

distraction—Something that makes it hard to pay attention.

harness—Leather straps with a U-shaped handle that the blind person holds to connect him to his guide dog.

mobility—The ability to move from one place to another.

obstacle—An object that stands in the way.

socialization—Training designed to help dogs be comfortable around many people.

trait—A quality that makes one dog different from another.

vaccinations—Shots that dogs need to protect against illness.

veterinarian—A doctor who takes care of animals.

Further Reading

Books

Hall, Becky. *Morris and Buddy: The Story of the First Seeing Eye Dog.* Morton Grove, Ill.: Albert Whitman & Co., 2007.

Patent, Dorothy Hinshaw. *The Right Dog for the Job: Ira's Path From Service Dog to Guide Dog.* New York: Walker & Company, 2004.

Schaefer, Lola M. *Some Kids are Blind.* Mankato, Minn.: Capstone Press, 2008.

Internet Addresses

American Humane Association
  <http://www.americanhumane.org>

Guide Dogs for the Blind
  <http://www.guidedogs.com>

The Seeing Eye
  <http://www.seeingeye.org/>

Index